Contents

Introduction 5

Foreword 9

–

Kiosks 16

–

Kiosk designers 204

Author 205

Acknowledgements 207

The Futuristic Face of Prefabrication

The industrialisation of building panel production and mass prefabrication reshaped architecture from the 1960s to the 1980s, especially in countries behind the Iron Curtain and, to a lesser extent, in the West. Throughout the second half of the 20th century, prefabrication emerged as a practical response to the perpetual housing shortage and unhurried reconstruction in the wartime aftermath. The traditional building industry struggled to meet the needs of rapidly expanding urban areas, their increasing populations, and the growing demand for services, commerce, and urban infrastructure.

As early as the beginning of the 20th century, Modernists recognised the potential of producing standardised elements in factories, which could then be efficiently assembled into buildings on-site. However, it wasn't until the manufacturing boom of the post-war decades, coupled with crucial sociopolitical policies, that prefabrication could become technically feasible on a mass scale.

While the former Eastern Bloc countries shared many similarities, the approach to prefab construction varied from country to country. In Poland, for instance, it dominated the housing sector above all. When viewed from a contemporary standpoint, its omnipresence, uniformity,

◁◁

Composition of cross-shaped K67 units and corridor elements. *Dahlia* flower shop, Ljubljana, Slovenia

◁

K67 kiosk interior, Ljutomer, Slovenia, 1969

and overwhelming scale are often met with aesthetic reservations. Nonetheless, it is essential to acknowledge that between 1950 and 1990, the construction of approximately 6.9-7.0 million apartments in Poland was largely facilitated by the so-called 'house factories'. The dominance of the large prefab panels was somewhat diminished by the crises of the 1980s, and the subsequent political transformation brought it to a definitive halt.

'The appearance of colourful kiosks made of innovative materials and textures popping up between the historic buildings and drab concrete housing estates brought a refreshing breeze of modernity and variety'

In neighbouring countries, prefabricated panel housing blocks were also extensively built, yet there were regions where modular structures took on diverse forms, scales, and functions. In 1966, Slovenian architect Saša J. Mächtig conceived a kiosk model designed for industrial production – lightweight yet functional – suitable for integration within the typically dense historic towns of Yugoslavia, particularly those frequented by tourists. This innovation was uniquely possible in Yugoslavia, which, in contrast to the Eastern Bloc, embraced a more progressive 'Western' ethos. The modular structure of a lightweight fibreglass booth seamlessly aligned with this modern 'vibe'.

The K67 kiosk emerged as the most renowned street modular structure, gaining recognition in the USA and Japan, and earning a place in the Museum of Modern Art. However, it was not the only one – similar standardised and mass produced kiosks were also developed in the USSR, GDR, and even in Finland (although they did not become widespread). Thanks to their modular construction, they could stand alone or be combined into rows, selling newspapers, drinks, acting as guard booths, tobacco kiosks, or cafés. Mirroring the fascination for space exploration in that era, streamlined fibreglass kiosks like the K67 also reflected the search for cosmic, futuristic forms, and reaching for less conventional materials.

In the latter half of the 20th century, Eastern Bloc cities were predominantly characterised by a grey aesthetic, with the architectural landscape dominated by the stern uniformity of 'brutalised' modernist forms. The appearance of colourful kiosks made of innovative materials and textures popping up between the historic buildings and drab concrete housing estates brought a refreshing breeze of modernity and variety, invoking very positive associations. Despite being standardised and serially produced, the booths disrupted the urban landscape's monotony with their diverse scales and forms.

Their presence, however, was not ubiquitous; modular kiosks were not widely popular in the Polish People's Republic or other Comecon countries until the 1980s, when cracks began to appear in the crumbling political system, allowing for pioneering economic activities. It turned out that the K67 and similar pavilions were perfectly suited for developing 'private initiative'. Consequently, companies that imported red and yellow poly-fibre kiosks to Poland, alongside locally manufactured systems, like the popular Kami, swiftly emerged. Thus, modular kiosks became emblems of the transformation era – a wholly distinct epoch, attesting to the universality of their designs.

Anna Cymer
Architectural historian and author based in Warsaw

Modular Timelessness

In the post-socialist era, kiosks – these unassuming structures of daily life – while not attaining the iconic status of monuments like Vera Mukhina's 'Worker and Kolkhoz Woman,' still constitute an equally vital element of our heritage and landscape. In the face of the socio-economic transformation that socialist countries underwent at the turn of the century, kiosks have emerged as crucial components of urban infrastructure, reflecting both economic pragmatism and ideological shifts.

Their design and implementation were not merely a response to consumer demands but also represented an effort to navigate swiftly changing realities where traditional forms of commerce were gradually proving insufficient. Despite their modest dimensions, kiosks played a role much larger than the sum of their physical components – they were miniatures of public spaces fostering new forms of social and economic interactions. Thus, they became labs for innovative design of usable space that encouraged experiments with materials, forms, and functions to offer solutions that were both adaptable and responsive to particular urban challenges.

The first and most iconic symbol of this creative and manufacturing revolution was the K67 kiosk designed by Saša J. Mächtig in 1966 as an answer to the escalating demand for modular and flexible usable spaces. Mächtig, a Slovenian architect and designer, envisioned a universal, easy-to-assemble, and mobile solution that could fulfil various urban functions. Production of the kiosk began in 1967 at the Imgrad factory in Ljutomer, Slovenia. The initial version of the K67 featured a uniform, monolithic structure, while the second generation, implemented to enhance production process and logistics, comprised several prefabricated elements. This evolutionary design facilitated even greater versatility, solidifying the K67's status as an icon of applied design.

On the wave of the popularity of standardised kiosks, other models emerged, including the Kiosk 190 series designed by Macedonian designer Aleksandar Nikoljski, who expanded on the concept of modularity, introducing the KC190 and KF190 models in the 1980s. Manufactured by the PVC company Treska Poliplast in Struga, Macedonia, these were marketed as adjustable, multi-functional units with myriad potential applications. From selling newspapers and tobacco to hosting lottery ticket sales, flower and souvenir shops, as well as artisanal and service businesses, the kiosk's modular character allowed for customisation based on location and function.

'Despite their modest dimensions, kiosks played a role much larger than the sum of their physical components – they were miniatures of public spaces fostering new forms of social and economic interactions'

While the KC190 bore resemblance to the K67 in shape, albeit with slightly different proportions and more varied tectonics, a less common but more eye-catching version featured large, oval windows reminiscent of space-age structures. Similar to the K67, Nikoljski's kiosks, owing to their functionality and adaptability, became integral elements of urban infrastructure, serving diverse purposes and enduring as parts of the former Yugoslavian landscape. However, unlike Mächtig's booths, their fame did not extend beyond Yugoslavia. Nonetheless, they enjoyed sufficient popularity in their domestic market for their designer to propose further systems, such as the K130, K260, and K520 series. Regrettably, these subsequent iterations failed to achieve the acclaim of the original concept, with the Treska Kiosk System from the early 1990s, and other projects, never progressing to mass production.

On the other hand, in socialist Central and Eastern Europe, monolithic kiosks put together using traditional techniques prevailed. They were typically constructed from metal, wood, or wood-derived materials. Modularity was often overlooked, with predominantly fixed freestanding structures dominating. As modernist urban planning of the Soviet era

Primary elements

1   Element A
2   Element B
3   Element C
4   Element D
5   Element E

Secondary elements

6   Door filler
7   Shop window filler
8   Sales window filler

Tertiary elements

9   Overhang
10   Shelf
11   Sales flap
12   Rubber seal
13   Glass

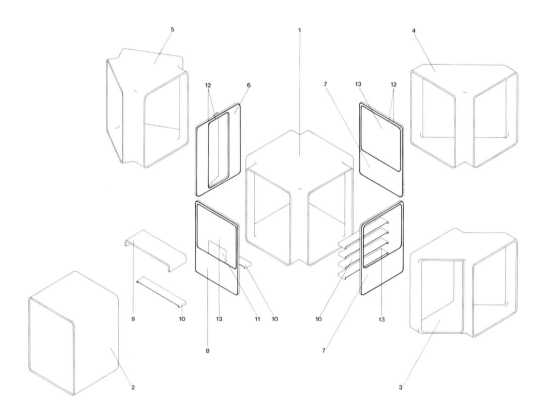

Decomposed axonometry of system K67 (1st
generation) by Saša J. Mächtig, 1967

RAZSTAVLJENA AKSO
NOMETRIJA
SISTEM K⁶⁷

failed to cater to small businesses with an adequate supply of business premises, kiosks became a significant, simple, yet effective way to foster the developing entrepreneurship that flourished with the advent of capitalism after the collapse of the USSR and the subsequent political-economic transformations.

In social landscapes transitioning from centrally planned to market economies, kiosks emerged as symbols of new opportunities for small entrepreneurs, enhancing local economic development and giving residents access to a wider range of products and services. They also led to notably easier logistics and cost reduction, revitalising urban spaces and rendering them more dynamic and diverse. The eventual emergence of small kiosk importers further fuelled this trend.

The heightened interest in Yugoslavian kiosks also prompted local companies with appropriate manufacturing capabilities to explore

◁⊼1

Peep show in Marszałkowska street,
Warsaw, 1993

△

Decomposed axonometry of system K67
(2nd generation) by Saša J. Mächtig, 1972

indigenous solutions. Concurrently, issues importing K67 kiosks arose amidst escalating conflicts in Yugoslavia, spurring the employment of alternative projects like the Kami kiosk, produced in Aleksandrów Łódzki, Poland. Although visually reminiscent of the K67, the Kami distinguished itself with more angular forms, eventually leveraging accusations of excessive similarity to Mächtig's design to its advantage. The versatility of its roof found applications beyond traditional kiosk functions, including bus stops or stadium stand coverings. Similarly, at the Polish Ustka shipyard, production commenced on KM63 kiosks featuring a distinctive hexagonal design, known as 'Ustka.' These kiosks could be interconnected into honeycomb-like modules, albeit achieving lesser popularity than other systems.

Another, but rather rare, example of modular urban architecture was the 'Bathyscaphe' – metal structures imported from the east, resembling angular deep-sea vehicles or diving suits. Although lacking an identifiable producer in the Soviet Union, these became landmarks, particularly in Ukraine and in Russian provinces. Irregular in size and often appearing makeshift, they nonetheless generally succeeded in fulfilling their basic functions. In recent years, however, Russian authorities began eradicating unauthorised 'Bathyscaphes' that were in random locations and visually polluting public spaces. As a result, many of these have now been put up for sale in local classifieds websites.

Yugoslavian kiosks, particularly the K67, attained significant prominence in global pop culture and public spaces, especially following their inclusion in the collection of the Museum of Modern Art (MoMA) in New York City. Their unique design and functionality also allowed for other creative uses of these mobile structures, from DJ consoles in Times Square to a popular café in Berlin, cementing the K67's iconic status and highlighting the universality and adaptability that paved the way for similar solutions implemented over the past few decades. Despite nearing its 60th anniversary, the kiosk continues to find utility across Europe, reaffirming its enduring relevance amidst cultural shifts and the passage of time, thereby continuing to inspire contemporary designers.

Maciej Czarnecki
Urban explorer and reporter based in Lower Silesia

PRODUCENT P/
P.P.H.U. KAMI
UL. WOJSKA P
95-070 ALEKSA
TEL/FAX (0-42)
MADE IN POLA

◁◁

From 2021 to 2024, a restored K67 (2nd
generation, element A), designed by Saša
J. Mächtig in the 1960s, served as both an
exhibit and a venue for civic activities as part
of an initiative by Avtomatik Delovišče, at
Anton Ukmar Square, Koper, Slovenia

△ | ▷

The Kami kiosk, named after its
manufacturer in Aleksandrów Łódzki,
was used as a parking lot booth until its
removal in 2023. Śródmiejska Dzielnica
Mieszkaniowa, aka 'Manhattan' Estate,
Łódź, Poland

This K67 (2nd generation, elements A+B) was formerly occupied by a bakery within Ogrody Estate, Ostrowiec Świętokrzyski, Poland

K67 (2nd generation, element B) in front of the 1967 Ljubljana Exhibition and Convention Centre in Bežigrad District, Ljubljana, Slovenia

∧ | ▷

Seasonal ice cream parlour K67 (2nd generation,
elements A+A) in Na Skarpie Estate, Toruń, Poland

◁◁ | △

Abandoned KC190 booth at the Higher Technical School of
Vocational Studies in the Pivara District of Kragujevac, Serbia.
This modular system was designed by Aleksandar Nikoljski
and manufactured in Macedonia in the 1980s

Modular kiosks for rent in Reinickendorf, Berlin, Germany. 'K67 Berlin' refurbishes, sells, and rents K67 kiosks, returning them to their original urban habitat

This modular system, known as 'Bathyscaphe', used to be imported from the former USSR, like the one in the car park at the lakeside in Borzygniew, Poland

UFO, a two-module 'Bathyscaphe', has been selling newspapers, cigarettes, cleaning products, cosmetics, and toys since the 1990s in the Wola District of Biała Podlaska, Poland

Deserted K67 primary module (2nd generation, element A) by the River Sava in Jakovo Suburb of Belgrade, Serbia

K67 (2nd generation, elements A+A) bakery in Gornji Grad, Belgrade, Serbia

Deserted K67 (2nd generation,
element A) in a quarry overlooking the
Štinjan cove in Pula, Croatia

Kami kiosk selling cigarettes and bus tickets in Dzierżoniów, Poland

KC190 kiosk (type KF) in the Maksimir District of Zagreb, Croatia

Coated Kami, which used to sell clothes, in front of the 1960s 'Sir Anatol's Hat' commercial pavilion. The kiosk was recently removed from Piastów-Kurak Estate, Łódź, Poland

Formerly used for selling cigarettes and household cleaning products, this K67 (2nd generation, element A) is currently inactive and leased as an advertising column in Żary, Poland

Derelict currency exchange Kami in Kudowa-Zdrój on the Polish-Czech border

Kami booth awaiting renovation on the premises of a road grill bar in the outskirts of Łódź, Poland

△ | ▷

This kiosk, which has been selling fresh farm eggs for over three decades, is part of a larger complex of second generation K67 booths in Świdnica, Poland. Ewa has been working here for the last four years

◁◁

K67 (2nd generation, element A) serving
as a watchtower at a motocross track in
the village of Židovinjak, Croatia

△ | ▷

Rotisserie chicken K67 (2nd generation,
element A) has been operational for thirty
years in Gryfino, Poland

A row of K67 kiosks (2nd generation, elements A+B), which previously sold eggs and vegetables, now have only one unit still operational, serving as a cigarette vendor, in Piaskowa Góra Housing Estate, Wałbrzych, Poland

SERWIS →
LAPTOPÓW

LAPTOPY
NA ZAMÓWIENIE

Different combinations of modular Kami used to serve as a greengrocer's and laptop repair point, Świebodzin, Poland

K67 (2nd generation, elements A+A) ice cream parlour on a beach, Skorzęcin Lake, Poland

An icon of Slovenian design, the refurbished K67 (2nd generation, element A) opens seasonally as a café at Ljubljana Airport, Slovenia

Abandoned K67 (2nd generation, element A) found in a car park in Powstańców Wielkopolskich Estate, Ostrów Wielkopolski, Poland

Abandoned K67 (2nd generation, element A) in front of the 1914 water tower at an open market in Żary, Poland

K67 (2nd generation, elements A+B) on the premises of the Squat and Cultural Centre Pekarna in the Magdalena District of Maribor, Slovenia

'Kolporter' newsstand K67 (2nd
generation, element A) in front
of a 1960s housing estate in the
centre of Pabianice, Poland

This K67 (2nd generation, element A), called 'Jugol' by its owner, Włodziu, was bought in the late 1990s to trade in all sorts of goods imported from Germany in Kamienna Góra, Poland

Parking lot K67 (2nd generation, elements A+A) at a hospital and medical university complex in the Savski Venac
District of Belgrade, Serbia

◁◁

The former Bar Slavček, a seven-module K67 (2nd generation), has recently been relocated from its original location on Jakčeva Street to Grm Castle in Novo Mesto, Slovenia, where it awaits renovation

△ | ▷

This K67 (2nd generation, elements A+B) was imported by Urszula and Stanisław from the former Yugoslavia thirty years ago and has since been used to provide key duplication services in the centre of Kielce, Poland

Newsstand Kami in the 1970s Kopernika Housing Estate, Legnica, Poland

K67 (2nd generation, elements A+B) in Grochów, Praga Południe District of Warsaw, Poland

Derelict 'Bathyscaphe' in a former car park at the foot of the Sudeten Mountains in Szklarska Poręba, Poland

'Bathyscaphe' at an open market on the Czech-Polish border in Kudowa-Zdrój used to sell plants and vegetables

KOT (2nd generation, elements A+B+A) in front of the 1972 Merkury shopping mall in the centre of Piła, Poland

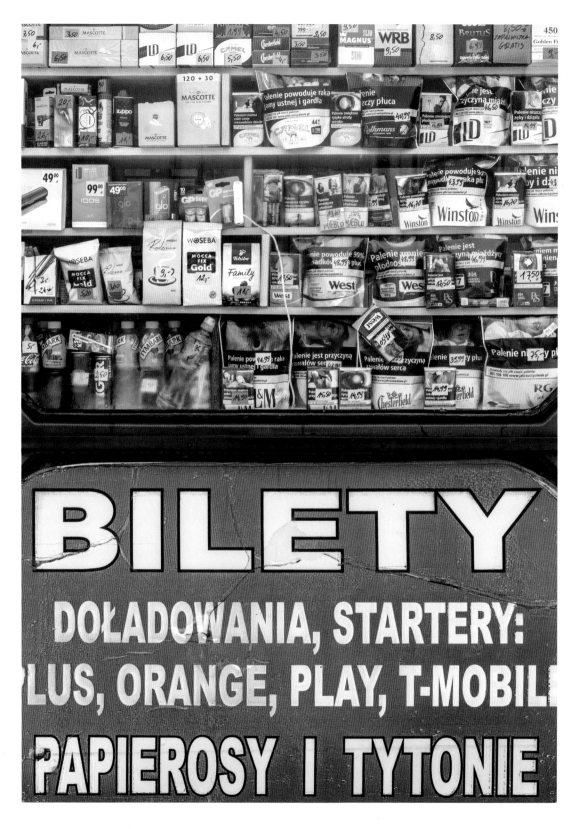

Public transport tickets, SIM cards, cigarettes, cold beverages, tea, coffee, stationary, cosmetics, batteries, and much more, can all be purchased in a Kami kiosk

Bimodular Kami 'Kolporter' newsstand and tobacconist in front of the Oncology Clinic in Nowy Fordon District, Bydgoszcz, Poland

⊲⊲ | △

Derelict gastronomical and grocery pavilion,
constructed from five connected K67 (1st generation,
elements A) in Górna District, Łódź, Poland

▷

A complex of K67 (2nd generation,
elements A) in the centre of
Świdnica, Poland

The XXL module K67 (2nd generation) has served as a grocery and liquor shop for twenty-five years in Przyjaźni Estate, Szczecin, Poland

Halina's K67 (2nd generation, element A) is a popular grilled chicken booth open year-round in Gryfino, on the Polish-German border

ГСП

БЕОГРАД

...ш осмех је мера нашег успеха

3211

Multimodular KC190 (type KF)
serving as a bus ticket vending
point in New Belgrade, Serbia

△ | ▷

Purchased thirty-four years ago for 70 million old Polish Zlotys,
this 'Tabak' K67 (2nd generation, element A) remains a popular
tobacconist in the Wrzeszcz District of Gdańsk, Poland

Kami used for storage on the side of the road in the village of Nasiegniewo, Kuyavian-Pomeranian Voivodeship, Poland

'Mini Menu' modular booth, designed by Zdzisław Wróblewski in the 1990s, serves as a warehouse for an adjacent shop in the central marketplace in Piła, Poland

◁◁

Two 'Krosno' type kiosks: a former ice-cream
parlour converted into a newsstand and a
temporarily closed booth in Jana Pawła II
Housing Estate, Sierpc, Poland

△ | ▷

Kioski is a second-generation K67
coffee shop. The booth was restored
by 'K67 Berlin' in 2018 and placed in
Kreuzberg, Berlin, Germany

The second-generation K67 modular kiosk entered serial production in the early 1970s by Imgrad, a manufacturer based in Ljutomer, Slovenia, until it was discontinued in the early 1990s

Restored K67 (2nd generation, element A) on the premises of The Museum of Architecture and Design in Ljubljana, Slovenia

The exhibition venue 'Nowy Złoty' K67 (2nd generation, elements A+B), originated in Wrocław and in 2021 was temporarily moved to the premises of Galeria Labirynt in Lublin, Poland

Ice-cream parlour K67 (2nd generation, elements A+B) opens seasonally next to the train station of Głogów, Poland

93

A row of K67 and Kami kiosks
sporadically open to sell fresh
eggs and fish in Tysiąclecia
Estate, Koszalin, Poland

A row of K67 (2nd generation, elements A) formerly used as newsstand and snack booths at the central Mali Park, overlooking the 1966 'Zastavin soliter' tower blocks, Kragujevac, Serbia

Abid has been serving shish kebab and hamburgers in his K67 (2nd generation, element A) for thirty-five years,
Stari Grad, Kragujevac, Serbia

◁◁

This Kami, located between the New
Cemetery and a coal heater contractor, opens
every day of the year to sell funeral wreaths
and grave candles in Radomsko, Poland

△ | ▷

Refurbished K67 (2nd generation, element A)
with convex glass slide panels recently placed
in the parking lot of the 1982 Delo Tower,
Bežigrad District of Ljubljana, Slovenia

K67 (2nd generation, element A) in front of Brvnara night club in the Trešnjevka – sjever District of Zagreb, Croatia

K67 (2nd generation, element A) metalworking shop guard booth in the Tezno District of Maribor, Slovenia

Zapiekanka and hot dogs have been the most popular fast food to be found in Polish booths

Abandoned fast food booth specialized in *zapiekanka* and waffles in Ostrowiec Świętokrzyski, Poland

Press booth K67 coated in corrugated steel panels in Na Skarpie Estate, Toruń, Poland

Derelict guard booth K67 (2nd generation, element A) at the tram depot in Blok 66 Estate, New Belgrade, Serbia

Trolleybus depot guard KC190 kiosk (type KB) in the Dorćol neighbourhood of Stari Grad, Belgrade, Serbia

◁◁

Local fast food K67 (2nd
generation, elements A+B)
booths in the city centre of
Kragujevac, Serbia

△ | ▷

Bimodular Kami, formerly offering sawing services,
has now been transformed into a CBD vending
machine and advertising pole in Słowackiego
Housing Estate, Piotrków Trybunalski, Poland

Bus ticket vending KC190 in the centre of Skopje, North Macedonia

Inactive K67 (2nd generation, elements A+B) at an open-air flea market in the Koło neighbourhood of Warsaw, Poland

A Kami used for booking Holy Mass intentions at Jasna Góra Monastery in Częstochowa, Poland

Bus stop featuring the rooftop panel designed by Kami in the Górna District of Łódź, Poland

OBIEKT
MONITOROWANY 24 h

◁◁ | △

Customised cluster of Kami
modules used as a car park
booth in Jasna Góra Monastery
in Częstochowa, Poland

▷

Kami kiosks were also used as police guard
booths in the 1990s, like this one, currently
serving as a warehouse for one of the stalls in
Bałucki Street Market in Łódź, Poland

'We recommend poultry offal' can
be read on this former butcher's K67
(2nd generation, elements A+B) at
1000-lecia Square, Głogów, Poland

Former hot dog K67 kiosk (2nd generation, element A) now serves shaved ice at the Ljubljana Central Market, Slovenia

Car park K67 booth (2nd generation, element A) in Šiška District, Ljubljana, Slovenia

Three connected Kami modules have been home to Edyta's florist's for over thirty years in Marysin Doły
neighbourhood, Łódź, Poland

K67 (2nd generation, elements A+B) at the Catholic Church Sanctuary of Our Lady Queen of Polish Martyrs opens
every Sunday to sell devotional objects, Praga Południe District, Warsaw, Poland

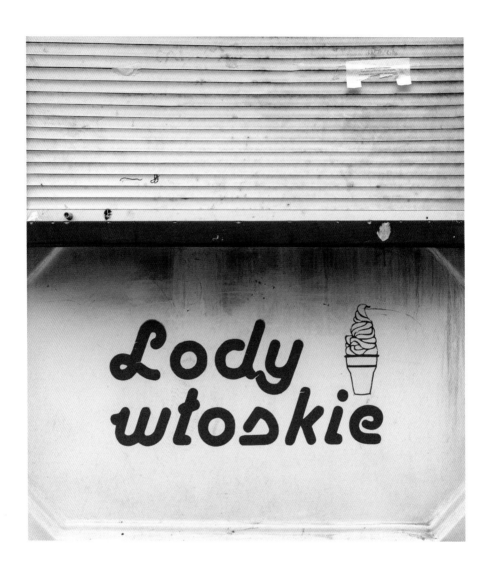

K67 (2nd generation, element A) used
as storage on a farm near Łacha Lake,
Józefów, Poland

△ | ▷

Former soft-serve ice cream and fast
food Kami in the centre of Głogow,
Poland, removed in 2024

Former 'Kolporter' Kami newsstand in the Trynek District of Gliwice, Poland

K67 kiosks, like this former fast food booth in the centre of Bydgoszcz, Poland, were popularly known as 'Jugokiosk'

Kami admission and ticket vending
booths at the city stadium in
Ostrowiec Świętokrzyski, Poland

Inoperative KC190 (type KF) at the rail tracks of the Skopje Central Train Station, North Macedonia

Fast food K67 (2nd generation, elements A+B) in the Jarše District of Ljubljana, Slovenia

◁◁

Two-module Kami lottery vending kiosk
in the 1970s Ogrody Housing Estate,
Ostrowiec Świętokrzyski, Poland

△ | ▷

'Warzywa i Owoce' greengrocer's
K67 (2nd generation, elements A+B)
in the centre of Jelenia Góra, Poland

140

KC190 (type KB) meteorological observation point at the Republic Hydrometeorological Institute of Serbia in Banovo Brdo, Belgrade, Serbia

Assembled out of four connected modules, this KC190 (type KF) serves as a bus ticket vending point in Blok 7a Estate, New Belgrade, Serbia

144   'Trafika' K67 magazine stand and tobacconist in the centre of Domžale, Slovenia

K67 (2nd generation, elements A+A) newsstand in Domžale, Slovenia

Former pastry shop bimodular
Kami near a *PKS* bus station in
Opole Lubelskie, Poland

Former coffee shop and bike service K67 (2nd generation, elements A+B) by the Danube River, New Belgrade, Serbia

Two single A modules of K67 (2nd generation) at a freight warehouse in the Tabor District of Maribor, Slovenia

◁◁

A row of five K67 (2nd generation, elements A) serving
as a currency exchange office, lotto point, and clothes
stalls in Narodnih Heroja Square, Kragujevac, Serbia

▷

Ticket vending KC190 (type KF)
at the Zagreb Hippodrome,
Novi Zagrob, Croatia

Kami newsstand and chemist's in
Słowackiego Housing Estate
in Piotrków Trybunalski, Poland

Anna sells grave candles at a Kami near the New Cemetery of Radomsko, Poland

Graveyard paraphernalia Kami in Stobiecko Miejskie Cemetery, Radomsko, Poland

Altered K67 (2nd generation, element A) factory office in Stare Bałuty neighbourhood, Łódź, Poland

Fast food K67 (1st generation, element A) in Zduńska Wola, Poland

Wojtek, Dorian, Daniel, and Robert
sell fruit and vegetable from this
XXL K67 in an open-air marketplace
in Świdnica, Poland

△ | ▷

The surroundings of the train and bus station in Krosno,
Poland, once boasted multiple K67 fast food booths.
Today, only two (2nd generation, elements A+B) are left,
closed down and awaiting imminent removal

'U Rycha' bar made of two modular booths near Świebodzki market, Wrocław, Poland

Parking lot K67 cabin (2nd generation, element A) in the Nadodrze neighbourhood of Wrocław, Poland

Former florist's and rotisserie
chicken K67 kiosks, inactive
since 2005, located in 'Na Kole'
open-air flea market in Wola
District, Warsaw, Poland

Multimodular Kami houses the 'Hell' rotisserie chicken in Słowackiego Housing Estate, Piotrków Trybunalski, Poland

K67 (2nd generation, elements A+B), recently removed from Piaskowa Góra Housing Estate, Wałbrzych, Poland

ZAPIEKANKI
HOT - DOGI

Former local fast food deli K67 (2nd generation, elements A+B) in Krosno, Poland

K67 (2nd generation, element A) 'Rosa' chain convenience store on the premises of the University Clinical Centre in Savski Venac District, Belgrade, Serbia

◁◁ | △

Abandoned K67 'Tisak' (2nd generation,
element A) on the premises of the 1972
Vjesnik publishing and printing house, closed
down in 2012, Trnje District, Zagreb, Croatia

▷

This bimodular kebab Kami has been
serving as a fast food booth at the
bus station in Bytom, Poland, since
the 1990s

K67-inspired modular booth near an empty warehouse in Rzgów, Poland

Warehouse K67 (2nd generation, element A) guard booth in the Tabor District of Maribor, Slovenia

24/7 car park Kami in Wesoła I neighbourhood, Kraków, Poland

K67 (2nd generation, element B) parking kiosk in Bródno neighbourhood, Warsaw, Poland

Former bakery K67 (2nd generation) transformed into a bag shop is open for business several days a week in the central marketplace of Piła, Poland

Former tobacconist and photocopy centre KC190 (type KF) in the Gazi Baba neighbourhood of Skopje, North Macedonia

A row of KC190 house a travel agency on the Vardar River embankment in central Skopje, North Macedonia

◁◁

A row of nine Kami, including a four-connected
module flower shop, set up in the 1990s in the
central market of Lubin, Poland

△ | ▷

Flower shop Kami selling funeral wreaths,
bouquets, and grave candles in front of the
New Cemetery in Radomsko, Poland

Convenience store and ticket vending Kami at a bus stop in downtown Wałbrzych, Poland

Abandoned 'Ruch' newsstand Kami in Jakubskie Przedmieście District, Toruń, Poland

This Soviet-era 'Bathyscaphe' has been in operation since the 1990s in Biała Podlaska, near the Polish-Belarusian border

Two-module Kami newsstand in the 1970s Tysiąclecia Państwa Polskiego Estate in Biała Podlaska, Poland

◁◁

A group of KC190 (type KF) kiosks which served
as ticket vending points and staff offices at the
Transportation Centre Skopje, North Macedonia,
designed by Kenzo Tange in the 1970s

△ | ▷

Two K67 *Menjačnica*, Serbian
for currency exchange office,
(2nd generation, elements A+B)
in Stari Grad, Kragujevac, Serbia

Abandoned bimodular KC190 booth in the Osogovo Mountains on the North Macedonian-Bulgarian border

Döner kebab K67 (2nd generation, elements A+A) on the side of a road in Neusalza-Spremberg, Germany

△ | ▷

Refurbished K67 (2nd generation, element
A) summer bar of Belgrade Urban Distillery in
Dorćol neighbourhood, Belgrade, Serbia

▷▷

This K67 (2nd generation, elements A+A)
has been home to a popular bakery in Gornji
Grad, Belgrade, Serbia, for fifty years

Locations

Germany ●

Berlin
Neusalza-Spremberg

Croatia ●

Pula
Zagreb
Židovinjak

North Macedonia ●

Kriva Palanka
Skopje

Serbia ●

Belgrade
Kragujevac

Slovenia ●

Domžale
Koper
Ljubljana
Maribor
Novo Mesto

Poland ●

Biała Podlaska
Borzygniew
Bydgoszcz
Bytom
Częstochowa
Dzierżoniów
Gdańsk
Gliwice
Głogów
Gryfino
Jelenia Góra
Józefów
Kamienna Góra
Kielce
Krosno
Koszalin
Kudowa-Zdrój
Kraków
Legnica
Lubin
Lublin
Łódź
Nasiegniewo
Opole Lubelskie
Ostrowiec Świętokrzyski
Ostrów Wielkopolski
Pabianice
Piła
Piotrków Trybunalski
Radomsko
Rzgów
Sierpc
Skorzęcin
Szczecin
Szklarska Poręba
Świdnica
Świebodzin
Toruń
Wałbrzych
Warszawa
Wrocław
Zduńska Wola
Żary

Kiosk Designers

Saša Janez Mächtig

Slovenian architect born in 1941 in Ljubljana known for his work in the field of industrial design. Starting with the polyester canopy of a café in Ljubljana, he went on to develop his seminal K67 kiosk. The first generation, designed in 1966, was included in the collection of the Museum of Modern Art (MoMA) in New York. The modular second generation was mass produced by Imgrad in Ljutomer, Slovenia, beginning in 1971 and then exported around the former Eastern Bloc. Mächtig has also developed other pieces of urban equipment such as waste bins, telephone booths, and bus stops and is currently working on the third generation of his famous kiosk.

Aleksandar Nikoljski

Architect and professor, born in 1937 in Peć, Kingdom of Yugoslavia (now Kosovo), he graduated from the University of Skopje in the early 1960s. Nikoljski specialized in interior and industrial design, notably creating the KC190 modular kiosk series in 1986, which was mass-produced by Treska Poliplast in Struga, Macedonia. In 1991, he co-developed the Treska Kiosk System. Nikoljski passed away in 2018.

Zdzisław Wróblewski

Industrial designer born in 1927 in Żuromin, Poland. Wróblewski worked for the Polish Institute of Industrial Design after graduating from the Academy of Fine Arts in Warsaw in 1954. He is best known for his modular interior and urban furniture designs allowing for the customisation of almost any space through numerous arrangements of various components. Some of those, such as the kiosk called 'Mini Menu', entered mass production in the early 1990s. Wróblewski died in Warsaw in 2019.

Author

Zupagrafika are David Navarro and Martyna Sobecka, an independent publisher, author and graphic design studio, established in 2012 in Poznań, Poland, celebrating modernist architecture, design and photography in a unique and playful way.

Over the last decade, David and Martyna have created, illustrated and published widely acclaimed books exploring the post-war modernist and brutalist architecture of the former Eastern Bloc and beyond, such as *Miasto Blok-How* (2012), *Blok Wschodni* (2014), *Blokowice* (2016), *Brutal London* (Prestel, 2016), *Brutal East* (2017), *The Constructivist* (2017), *Modern East* (2017), *Brutal Britain* (2018), *Hidden Cities* (2018), *Panelki* (2019), *Eastern Blocks* (2019), *Concrete Siberia* (2020), *Brutal Poland* (2020), *Monotowns* (2021), *Brutal East vol. II* (2021), *The Tenants* (2022), *Soviet Playgrounds* (2022), *Słup* (2023), *Brutalia* (2023), *Concrete Hong Kong* (2023).

Kiosk is a photographic exploration of the remaining modernist kiosks scattered around the former Eastern Bloc and ex-Yugoslav countries. Mass-produced from the 1970s to the 1990s, modular systems like the seminal K67, the Polish Kami, the Macedonian KC190, and the Soviet 'Bathyscaphe' could be found anywhere from bustling city squares to socialist-era housing estates. Some remain active or have been refurbished while others have been abandoned and are slowly fading from the urban landscape.

Acknowledgements

Zupagrafika would like to thank Saša J.Mächtig, Tomaž Mächtig, Maciej Czarnecki, Anna Cymer, Museum of Architecture and Design MAO Ljubljana (Špela Šubic, Maja Vardjan, Tanja Vergles), Martin and Taro (K67 Berlin), Max Beauchez, k67.belgrade, Alexander Veryovkin, Paquita Borque, Maciej Kabsch, Marta, Maciej & Grusia Mach, Kasia & Paweł, Andrés & Judit, Rita & Simón, for their help and support.

Design, edition, captions, concept:
David Navarro & Martyna Sobecka (Zupagrafika)

Photography:
David Navarro & Martyna Sobecka / Zupagrafika (pp. 16-201)

Introduction:
Anna Cymer

Foreword:
Maciej Czarnecki

Archive Photos:

Saša J. Mächtig / MAO Collection (pp. 2-3, 8, 11, 14)
Janez Kališnik / MAO Collection (p. 4)
Sławomir Kamiński / Agencja Wyborcza.pl (pp. 12-13)

Published by Zupagrafika
Poznań, Poland. 2024

Printed in Poland
Paper from responsible sources
ISBN 978-83-963268-6-7
www.zupagrafika.com